The Story of

SPACE

& ROCKETS

Written and illustrated by Roger Arno,
Official Artist for the Apollo-Soyuz Recovery
Aerospace engineer, NASA

No one knows who invented the rocket. We do know that gunpowder was invented by the Chinese. Perhaps the first rocket was an accidentally ignited container of this black powder. By 1200 A.D. fire arrows—common arrows with strap-on boosters (1)—were in widespread use in China. When it was discovered that the feathers were not needed, they were eliminated, leaving the rocket and guide-stick design still found in fireworks today.

Rockets improved by manufacturing technique (2) continued to be used for military purposes and fireworks. It was the British bombardment of Fort McHenry in Baltimore during the War of 1812 that gave Francis Scott Key the inspiration to write of "the rockets' red glare." These rockets were difficult to aim accurately and were more useful at scaring enemy soldiers and horses than injuring them.

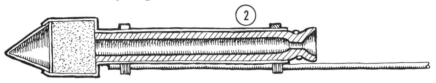

Early concepts of spaceflight were based not on rockets but on harnessed geese, balloons, sailing ships, antigravity material, and even bottles of rising dew. Most visionaries did not realize the enormous amount of energy required to escape the Earth's gravity. If Jules Verne's heroes in *From the Earth to the Moon* (1865) had really achieved the necessary escape velocity of 25,000 miles per hour in a one-mile-long cannon, they would have been squashed flat by the tremendous acceleration.

Rockets can limit acceleration forces by what might be thought of as controlled explosion. When fuel burns, gasses expand in all available directions. In an ordinary cannon (3), when the gunpowder goes off, the gasses push in all directions. The cannon barrel contains the side thrusts; the forward thrust pushes the cannonball out of the barrel, while the rearward thrust causes the cannon barrel to recoil.

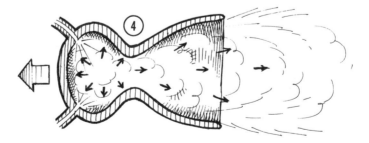

If there were no cannonball, the burning of the gunpowder would expel gases from the barrel and the cannon would still recoil. If we designed a very light barrel and fed fuel into it continuously, we would have a rocket motor (4).

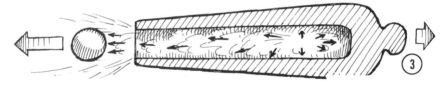

The idea of using rockets for space flights was first suggested in 1883 by Konstantin Eduardovich Tsiolkovsky, a Russian born in 1857. In 1903 he conceived of fueling a rocket with liquid hydrogen and liquid oxygen—the same fuel-oxidizer combination that would power part of the Saturn moon rocket sixty years later. He even realized that multi-stage rockets might help attain escape velocity. However, the materials and guidance technology did not yet exist to make his ideas a practical reality.

Dr. Robert Goddard, an American born in 1882, made the first working liquid-fueled rocket. On March 16, 1926 the rocket shown on this page reached a height of 40 feet while travelling 184 feet to a landing in a cabbage patch. Goddard had little money, and had to use material scavenged from junk piles for many of his later experiments, despite some funding from the Smithsonian Institution and Daniel Guggenheim. As a result, some of his rockets were too heavy to fly. But by 1935 he had a fifteen-foot rocket with a fuel-pumping system which climbed a mile and a half and reached a speed of 700 miles per hour. Later he developed a system to stabilize the rocket with a gyroscope, and by 1942 Goddard and his assistants had a rocket almost identical in design to the German V-2, though only a fraction of its size—too small for the army to consider it practical. Goddard died in 1945.

After Germany's defeat in World War I, the peace treaty restricted German development of aircraft and artillery. As there were no restrictions on research in rocketry, research funds went there, starting in the late 1920's. The program which led to the V-2 rocket, with General Dornberger and Wernher von Braun, started in 1932, and launched its first successful V-2 on October 3, 1942. The rocket reached a record altitude of 56 miles and a maximum speed of 3350 miles per hour in 45° flight after a vertical takeoff. It fell 119 miles away.

Rockets had no significant effect on the outcome of World War II, but the intercontinental ballistic missiles and space launch vehicles of today are just further developments of the rockets designed by the Germans and Dr. Goddard.

Before the end of World War II over 5000 V-2's were produced. They weighed 12½ tons, of which 8300 pounds was methyl alcohol fuel (1), and 11,000 pounds liquid oxygen (2). Graphite steering vanes (3) guided the rocket by deflecting the exhaust gases as they came from the combustion chamber (4). Elevator controls in the tail fins aided in guidance. The nose of the 46-foot missile was a one-ton bomb (5). Immediately below it was the gyroscopic guidance system, which could be equipped to report the rocket's location in flight by radio. The fuel and oxidizer turbopumps (6) were powered by a hydrogen peroxide steam generator (7).

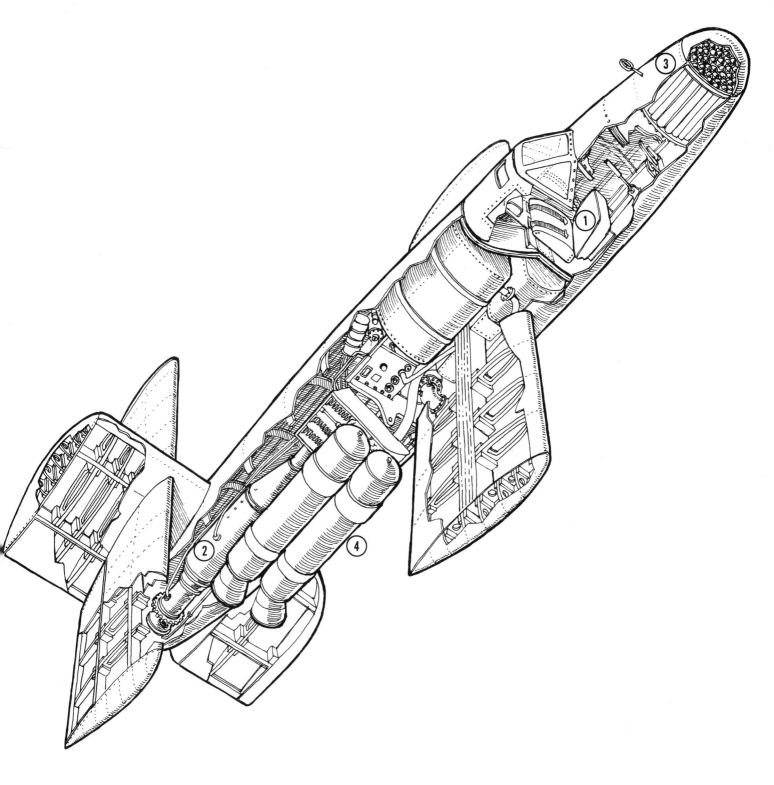

In response to Allied air raids on German industry, the Germans worked to develop deadly anti-aircraft devices. One such device was a rocket plane, the BACHEM Bp8-348 NATTER, a single-seat (1) interceptor, powered by a rocket engine (2), and armed with a battery of rockets (3) to fire into formations of Allied bombers. The NATTER was to be controlled from the ground by an anti-aircraft superintendent, launched vertically from a ramp with the aid of auxiliary rockets (4), flying almost straight up to intercept bombers. When the pilot spotted approaching bombers, he would take control, fly close to them, fire his 24 73-millimeter rockets, and glide away at about 150 miles per hour. Then he would jettison the forward part of the craft, and the main body and the pilot would parachute to the ground separately.

The NATTER was 21 feet, 3 inches long, and designed with a wooden frame for cheap and quick assembly. Two hundred were ordered, but by the time the war ended only one test flight had been made. The results were disastrous.

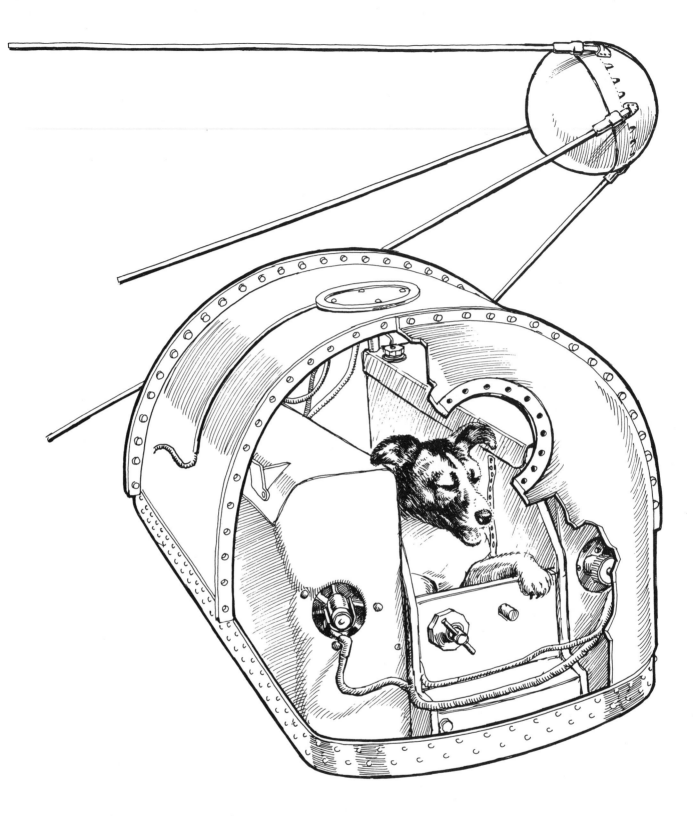

When World War II ended, the United States and the Soviet Union collected German rocket experts and their rockets, and continued research. On October 4, 1957 the Soviet Union stunned the world by launching the first artificial satellite, Sputnik, shown above. It weighed 184 pounds—ten times the weight of Explorer 1, the first U.S. satellite, which was not launched until January 31, 1958.

Before the first U.S. satellite went up, the Russians put Sputnik II in orbit: a pressurized container which housed the dog Laika with a controlled atmosphere, food supply, waste collection system, and biological sensors. Sputnik II weighed over half a ton, and kept Laika alive 8 days, until the oxygen supply ran out November 11, 1957.

Sputnik III, a cone-shaped flying laboratory weighing 2916 pounds, went up May 15, 1958. Obviously the Russians had developed the huge boosters required to deliver heavy payloads — or nuclear warheads. But it was ten years before the West got a look at the impressive design of this Vostok launch vehicle.

The Vostok launch vehicle has been the workhorse of the Soviet space program. The 125-foot long rocket is capable of putting over 10,000 pounds into Earth orbit or sending 1000 pounds beyond the Earth's gravitational hold. The central core of the rocket has two stages. It is surrounded by four booster sections, each of which has four main engines like the central first stage. The 20 rocket motor combination provides a total thrust of over one million pounds, burning liquid oxygen and kerosene. A total of twelve smaller (vernier) motors pivot to provide steering.

World War II provoked many developments in aviation. New technology led to new goals—such as developing aircraft able to exceed the speed of sound. Sound waves travel at 760 miles per hour at sea level at 75°F, and somewhat slower at higher altitudes where the atmosphere is thinner. Only bullets had ever gone this fast.

The rocket-powered U.S. X-1 was ordered in February 1945. On October 14, 1946 it cracked the sound barrier, reaching the speed of 946 miles per hour. The little X-1 carried so little fuel that it was dropped into flight from beneath the wing of a B-29 bomber to avoid wasting fuel for take-off. It reached a record altitude of 98,400 feet in 1954; on December 12, 1953 Captain Charles "Chuck" Yaeger reached 1612 miles per hour in it—almost 2½ times the speed of sound.

The most famous rocket-powered plane is the X-15 shown here. On September 17, 1959 a B-52 dropped the X-15 from under its wing for the first flight. It reached 2.3 times the speed of sound. By 1966 it reached 4,223 miles per hour, flying 67 miles high, at the fringes of space. A typical mission flight profile is shown below. Three of the X-15's pilots, Joe Walker, Robert White, and Neil Armstrong, became astronauts.

An object in orbit must travel rapidly enough not to be pulled down by gravitational attraction, but not so rapidly that it flies off at a tangent. Planetary orbits, like those of artificial satellites, are ellipses. This means an Earth satellite can maintain a constant altitude or the altitude can be made small on one side of the Earth and large on the other.

The closer a satellite is to the body it orbits, the faster it must travel. A satellite in this low orbit (1), shown originating from Kennedy Space Center, would circle the Earth in 90 minutes or so, traveling at a speed of about 18,000 miles per hour. The higher orbit (2), shown originating at the Vandenburg launch complex on a North-South pass, is called a polar orbit. It can be adjusted to keep a constant angle with the Sun as the Earth turns beneath (i.e., "sun synchronous"). A satellite in orbit at 23,000 miles above the Earth travels at about 7,000 miles per hour and has a period of 24 hours—which means it will remain over the same area of the Earth as the Earth rotates (i.e., "geosynchronous") (3).

The first U.S. satellite, Explorer 1, discovered radiation bands surrounding the Earth, a double band of charged particles trapped by the Earth's magnetic field. These are known as the Van Allen Radiation Belts, and are primarily protons and electrons emitted by the Sun along with such electromagnetic radiations as light and heat.

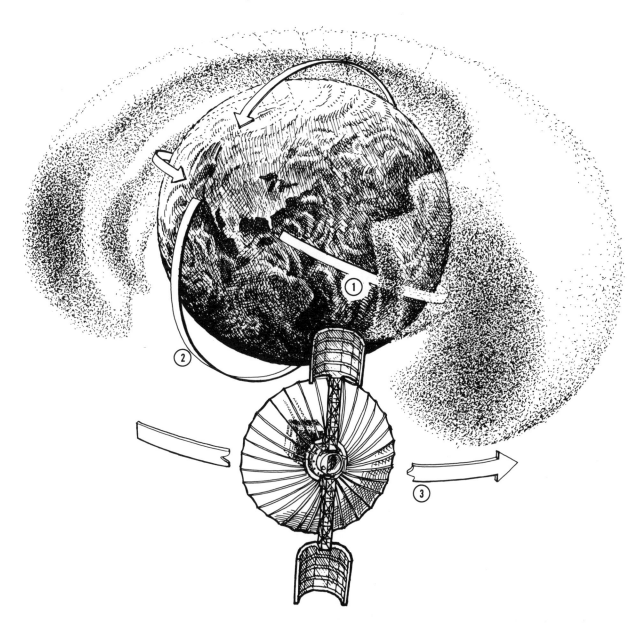

On April 12, 1961 a Soviet rocket put a man in orbit about the Earth for the first time. Major Yuri Gagarin circled the Earth once in 108 minutes, then landed a few hundred miles from his launch point at the Baikonur cosmodrome.

Gagarin's satellite was a cramped sphere, 7½ feet in diameter (1), coated with an ablation material—a substance intended to burn away when the friction produced by the satellite's reentry into the atmosphere produced great heat. Most of the heat is carried away with the burning material.

Inside were food and water, a sanitary system, equipment to regulate the air supply, a clock, a radio, a television camera to send pictures back to the U.S.S.R., an emergency heat regulation system, landing system radar, a landing parachute, and a manual control stick. Gagarin sat in an ejection seat mounted on rails.

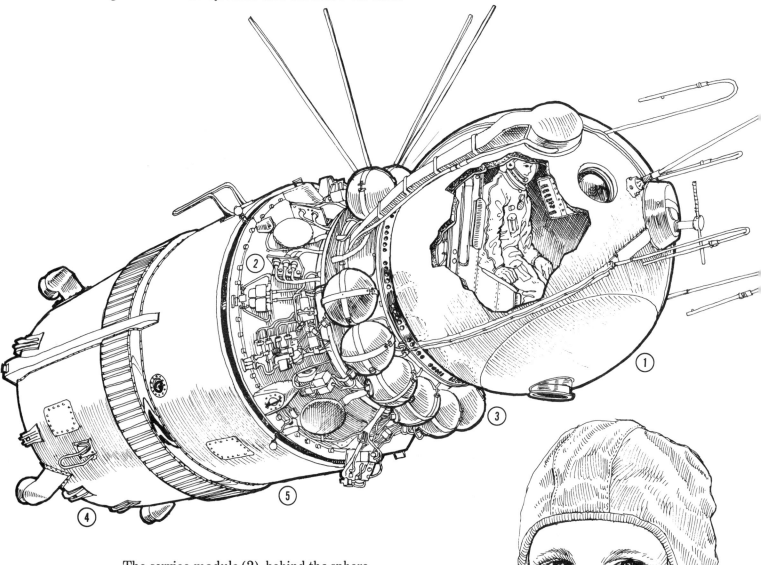

The service module (2), behind the sphere held oxygen and nitrogen bottles (3) for breathing, chemical batteries to supply electrical power, and UDMH and nitric acid fuels for orientation control. Behind the service module a propulsion stage (4) was attached with a skirt (5). The skirt encloses the rocket motor used to slow Gagarin's capsule for reentry. The rocket motor and service module are jettisoned before reentry.

The Jet Propulsion Laboratory operates this 210-foot diameter antenna for NASA. This antenna and others like it in Spain and Australia allow any spot in the sky to be covered continuously as the Earth turns. They track objects sent into space, receiving radio communications from them and sending instructions to them. These antennas are so sensitive they can detect a signal so weak it would take millions of years to gather the energy to light a nightlight for one thousandth of a second.

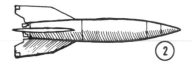

①

②

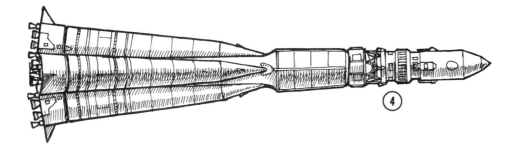

③

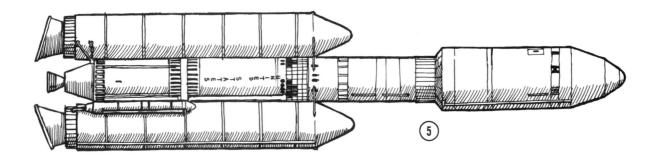

④

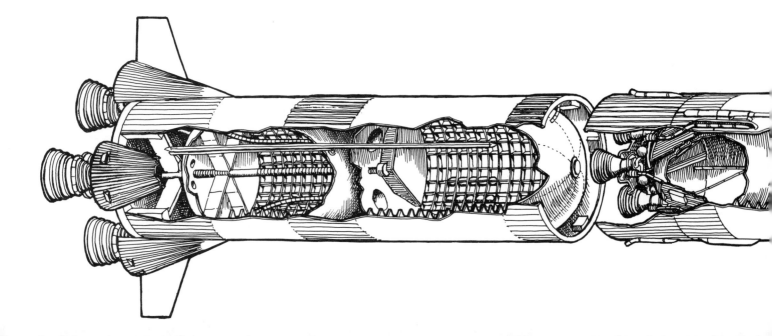

⑤

In the 40 years between Goddard's first liquid-fuel rocket (1) and the Saturn V (6), the rocket has grown immensely in size: the Saturn rocket which carried the first men to the Moon was four times as long as the ship that brought Columbus to the New World.

The rocket has grown because larger rockets can carry more or go further. But to get off the ground a rocket must have a thrust greater than its total weight. The larger the rocket, the greater the thrust needed. The Saturn V first stage weighs 187,574 pounds *empty*: it burns over 4.6 million pounds of kerosene and liquid oxygen in 127 seconds, developing 7.7 million pounds of thrust in the process. Before the fuel is burned up the rocket must reach its desired speed and trajectory.

This table compares characteristics of some important rockets.

SOME ROCKETS AND LAUNCH VEHICLES

Name	Country	First Flight	Liftoff Weight (lb)	Payload (lb)/Orbit	Length (ft)	Number Stages	Fuel Type	Mission Notes
② V-2	Germany	1942	25,000	2,000/ —	46	1	liquid ox. alcohol	Ballistic missile
③ Atlas	USA	1959	269,000	2-3,000/low	71 to 87 w/payld.	1½ + payload	liquid ox. kerosene	Mercury, science, military (converted ICBM)
Atlas Centaur	USA	1966	326,000	11,200/low 4,000/geosynch 1,300/escape	131	2½	liquid ox. kerosene hydrogen	OSO, Intelsat IV, Surveyor Mariner, Pioneer 10, 11
Delta (Thor)	USA	1960	295,000	4,500/low 1,500/geosynch 850/escape	116	3	liquid ox. kerosene solid strap-ons	Landsat, Goes, SMS, etc. many communication and resource satellites
Scout	USA	1960	47,000	390/low	75	4	solid	Research payloads
⑤ Titan IIIE Centaur	USA	1974 (IIIC 1965)	1,400,000	38,000/low 8,000/escape	160	3	liquid,solid strap-ons, liq. ox. hydrogen	Viking (Gemini, Titan II)
Saturn 1B	USA	1966	1,300,000	40,000/low	225 with Apollo CSM	3	liquid ox. kerosene	Apollo
⑥ Saturn V	USA	1967	6,300,000	285,000/low 100,000/Moon	363 with Apollo	3	liquid ox. kerosene hydrogen	Apollo, Skylab
Shuttle	USA	1981	4,400,000	60,000/low 30,000/polar	184	2	liquid ox. hydrogen	Multi-purpose, 60 ft x 15 ft dia bay
Cosmos	USSR	1962	60,000	900/low	105	2-3	liquid	Cosmos, Intercosmos
④ Vostok	USSR	1957		10,400/low 1,000/escape	125	2½	liquid ox. kerosene	Sputnik, Vostok
Soyuz	USSR	1960	720,000	16,500/low 3,640/escape	167	2½	liquid	Voskhod, Soyuz, Luna Cosmos, Venera, Mars
Proton	USSR	1965		38,000/low 12,000/escape	155	3-4	liquid	Proton, Salyut, Zond Luna 15/16, Mars

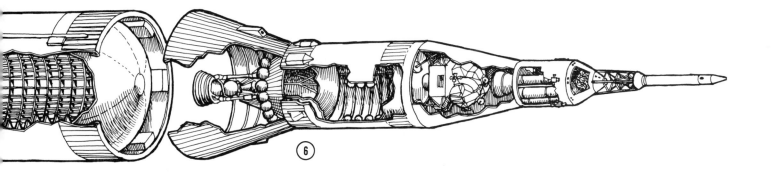

After the first U.S. manned spaceflights in the Mercury series came the Gemini Program. These cramped two-man capsules logged 2000 man-hours in space in ten flights, provided experience in space rendezvous and docking, and confirmed man's ability to tolerate long periods of weightlessness in space.

The front compartment of the Gemini spacecraft houses the rendezvous radar (1), drogue parachute (2), main parachute (3), and reentry attitude thrusters (4). Behind the manned compartment, in the retromodule, are the retro-rockets (5) and maneuvering thrusters (6). The last section, the equipment module, contains additional fuel and oxidizer storage, and attitude control thrusters (7). Gemini spacecraft were launched by the Titan II rocket.

On June 3, 1965 astronaut Edward H. White became the first American to walk in space. Connected to the Gemini IV spacecraft by a 25-foot umbilical line (8) and a tether, he tested an experimental propulsion unit for work outside in space (9). The pack on his chest contained an eight-minute emergency oxygen supply (10).

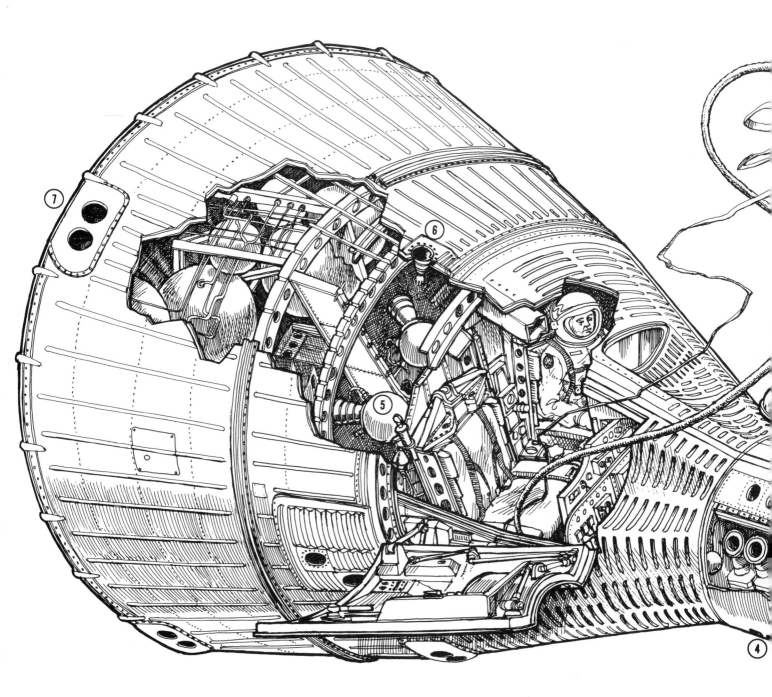

The Gemini IV flight in 1965 and later missions have been controlled from this Mission Control Center at NASA's Johnson Space Center near Houston, the nerve center of one of the most advanced computer complexes in the world. A global communications and tracking network provides information. During a mission, four teams alternate on duty, monitoring all information reported. At the control consoles are a Flight Director, a Booster Systems Engineer, a Retrofire and Abort Manager, a Flight Dynamics Officer (responsible for trajectory, maneuvers, and onboard propulsion), a Network Controller, a Flight Activities Officer, a Public Affairs Officer, a Director of Flight Operations, a NASA Headquarters Mission Director, a Defense Department representative, and an Experiments Officer. In case of problems, many other individuals are on call within the building and around the world.

APOLLO MISSION PROFILE

Arthur C. Clarke, the science fiction writer, suggested the concept of the communications satellite in the late 1940's. Within 20 years his idea became a reality. These satellites receive and retransmit radio signals—telephone calls, television programs, or other data. Usually they maintain a geosynchronous orbit, in continuous view from the same spot on the ground.

The Marisat (Maritime Satellite), here being tested in a noise-absorbing test chamber, helps ship-to-shore communications. In orbit it is spin-stabilized: the lower cylindrical body spins on a vertical axis while the system of antennas on top remains stationary. There are three large helical UHF antennas, four small helical L-band antennas, and a pair of C-band horn antennas for wide-angle coverage. The UHF provides one voice and 44 teletype channels or 14 voice channels. Seven thousand solar cells covering the cylindrical body supply 330 watts of power as they rotate into the Sun's rays. Three Marisats were launched in 1976: at 23,000 miles altitude they cover the Atlantic, Pacific, and Indian Oceans.

Here on a test stand (1) is the third Landsat satellite. In orbit, the solar arrays (2) face the sun to generate electrical power for the Earth observation sensors below (3) and the orientation equipment above (4).

From its 570-mile high sun synchronous orbit, Landsat transmits agricultural, geological and other ground cover information as a series of picture elements. The elements can be used to construct conventional pictures or coded images as shown.

Typical Landsat Satellite Image Data

```
G G G G G G G G G W W G G 1 1 1 1 ⊠ ⊠
G G G G G G G G W W W G G G 1 1 ⊠ 1 1 1
G G G G G G G G W W W W G G 1 ⊠ 1 1 1
G G G G G G G G W W W W W G 1 ⊠ 1 1 1 1
G G / / / / G G W W W W W G 1 ⊠ 1 1 1 W
G G / / / / G W W W W W W 1 ⊠ ⊠ 1 1 1 W
G G / / / / G W W W W W W 1 ⊠ 1 1 1 1 W
G G / / / / G G G W W W 1 ⊠ ⊠ 1 1 1 1 1
```

In the continuing dream of man's conquest of space, the Skylab Project represented a significant step toward a continuously habitable space station. In three missions of 28, 59, and 84 days duration, the 100-ton, 22-foot diameter, 118-foot long orbiting laboratory provided the opportunity to evaluate the physiological effects of the space environment over extended periods. In addition, experiments in solar astronomy, Earth observation, and space manufacturing were conducted.

The 2.5 billion dollar project was nearly aborted when, during launch with a Saturn V rocket on May 14, 1973, atmospheric drag tore away a thin meteoroid shield that was wrapped around the converted Saturn IVB rocket stage laboratory (1). In the process, one large solar panel was torn loose and flung into space (2) while its mate on the opposite side was entangled and prevented from deploying. Once in orbit, some 270 miles above the Earth's surface, the solar panels attached to the Apollo Telescope Mount unfurled as programmed (3), but inside the laboratory temperatures soared to 300° F because the missing outer layer had caused a great shift in the delicate balance in the heat exchange with the Sun's unfiltered rays.

While film, chemicals, and medical supplies were being destroyed in the laboratory, only quick thinking and a makeshift parasol (4) carried aloft by the delayed first crew saved the laboratory from becoming a worthless derelict.

The final three-man crew opened the airlock door (5), floated through the multiple docking adapter (6), settled into their Apollo spacecraft (7), and left the station on February 8, 1974, having brought the total manned occupation to some 2,476 orbits.

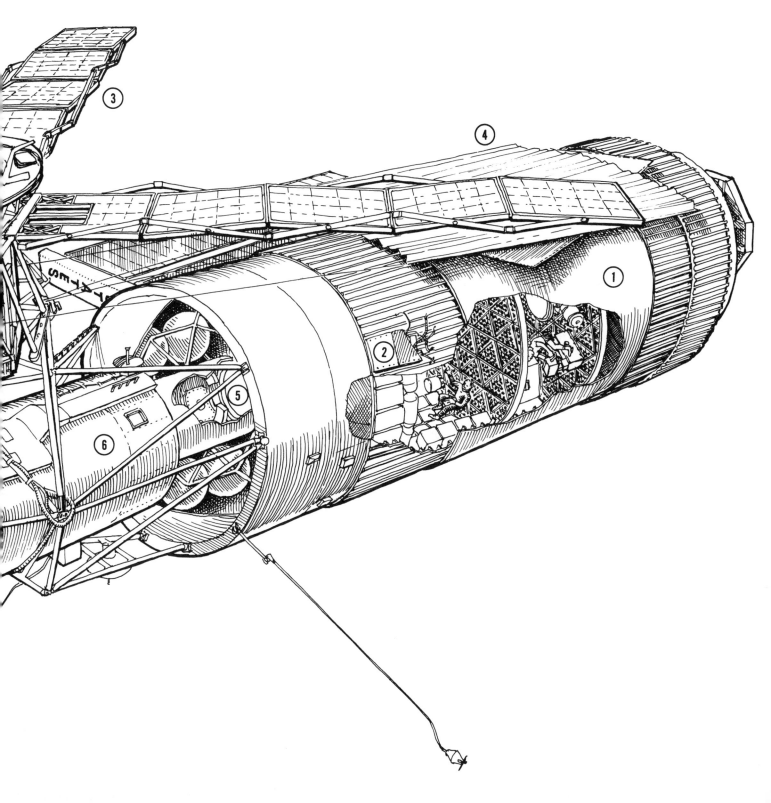

The Apollo-Soyuz Test Project was the first U.S.-U.S.S.R. cooperative manned space venture. The mission began on July 15, 1975 when Aleksei Leonov and Valeri Kubason blasted off from the Soviet cosmodrome. Seven hours later the American crew of Thomas Stafford, Vance Brand, and Donald (Deke) Slayton was launched from the Kennedy Space Center. The two spacecraft rendezvoused on July 17 and remained docked for two days. Link-up was accomplished via the 10-foot long, 5-foot diameter docking adapter which acts as an airlock. This allowed the transfer of men between the five pounds per square inch pure oxygen atmosphere of the Apollo spacecraft to the 10 pounds per square inch oxygen-nitrogen mixture in the Soyuz. The Soviet spacecraft atmosphere had been reduced from its usual 14.7 pounds per square inch for this particular mission. The Soyuz craft returned to Earth on July 21; the Apollo spacecraft splashed down in the Pacific Ocean three days later on July 24. This was the first mission to be televised live in the Soviet Union.

The Apollo-Soyuz mission was never touted as one of great scientific significance, but it did provide unique opportunities for scientists of both countries to observe the hardware and methods of the other. The Mission was also a demonstration of the potential for international cooperation in space, and it opened the door to the possibility of orbital rescue in the event of mishap at some future date.

Despite the difficulties that might have occurred due to poor weather, launch delays, or other technical problems, the two-and-a-half years of planning paid off. The mission was completed exactly according to schedule. However, tragedy was narrowly averted at the close of the mission when the Apollo crew was accidentally exposed to reaction control fuels during reentry. The U.S. astronauts were immediately quarantined aboard the recovery ship and remained confined for several weeks in Hawaii until the danger of lung infection had passed.

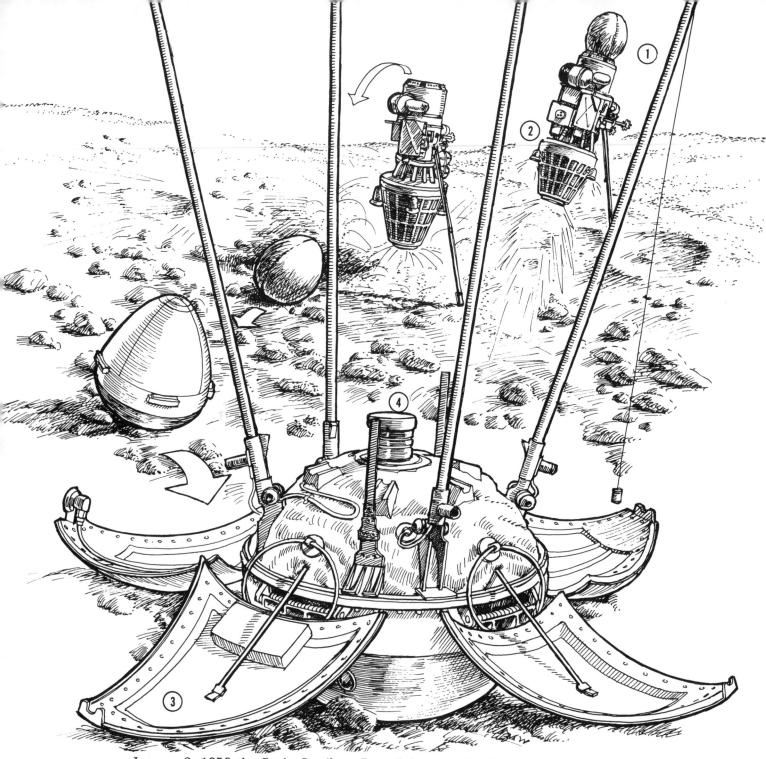

January 2, 1959 the Soviet Lunik, or Luna 1, became the first spacecraft to escape Earth's gravity. The 797-pound probe passed within 3700 miles of the Moon, which it was probably intended to hit. On September 12, 1959 Lunik 1, weighing 860 pounds, became the first man-made object to hit the Moon. Lunik 3, launched October 4th, managed to photograph the Moon's hidden backside. The spin-stabilized spacecraft's rotation was stopped during the long curved path behind the Moon while a series of pictures were taken on 35 millimeter film with two telephoto lenses. The film was then developed, the images scanned electronically, and the data transmitted back.

After several unsuccessful attempts, Luna 9, launched January 31, 1966, achieved the first controlled landing on the Moon. The 3490-pound spacecraft had two parts: a 220-pound egg-shaped instrument capsule (1) sat atop a rocket stage and service compartment (2), from which it was ejected during landing. Weight distribution and four unfurling petals (3) settled it bottom down to expose the instruments, antenna, and the television camera (4) which took the first photographs from the Moon's surface.

The Russians may never have intended to send men to the Moon, but they carried out a comprehensive program of lunar exploration, starting with fly-bys and orbiters, and continuing to landers, rovers, and sample returns. The first Lunokhod rover landed aboard the Luna 17 in November 1970 and operated almost a year, covering 6 miles before the isotope heater failed, allowing its internal systems to freeze. Lunokhod 2, on Luna 21, touched down in the Sea of Serenity January 16, 1973 and operated into July, surviving four lunar day-night cycles and traveling 23 miles.

The Lunik descent vehicle unfolded twin ramps so that blockage of one could not immobilize the Lunokhod. A five-man crew controlled the 1840-pound rover from Earth, with data and television links through an omnidirectional low gain antenna (2) and a high gain narrow-beam directional antenna (3). The vehicle is a circular pressurized instrument compartment supported by eight independently powered wire mesh wheels. The insulated convex top (1) is a lid: it opens 180° to the rear on hinges to expose energy-gathering solar cells to the 340-hour lunar day. The four-foot four-inch high vehicle has twin television cameras (4) as well as a wide-angle camera. Toward the rear is a soil probe and an odometer wheel (5).

The U.S. obtained lunar surface images from the series of Ranger spacecraft just prior to their impact on the lunar surface. This was followed by Lunar Orbiter which took extensive lunar photos for complete surface mapping. The next step in preparing for a manned landing was to place instruments there with a controlled, or "soft", landing. The Surveyor craft, here shown approaching the Moon, was 10 feet high and weighed 2285 pounds. As it approached, it slowed by firing the main retro-rocket (1). The 36-inch diameter spherical retro-rocket comprised more than 60% of the craft's weight; after it had been fired, radar attached to the end of the rocket nozzle (2) triggered explosive bolts and it was jettisoned.

Vernier rockets (3) stabilized the craft while the retro-rocket was firing, then slowed it to 3 miles an hour and brought it within 14 feet of the surface. Three honeycomb blocks (4) and three honeycomb pads on the landing gear (5) cushioned the touchdown. Surveyor 1 made a successful soft landing on the Moon June 1, 1966.

Its television camera (6) could take 200- and 600-line TV pictures. In the following six weeks, it took 11,150 photos, which were transmitted through low gain antennas (7) or the high gain planar antenna (8), with the power supplied by a solar array of 1960 solar cells (9). An extendable arm with a scoop (10) tested soil hardness and texture; an alpha-scattering instrument gave the first evaluation of the lunar soil chemical composition.

Surveyor 6 was the first craft to lift off the lunar surface, using its vernier rockets for a short hop. Surveyor 7 was the last of the series.

On July 20, 1969 Apollo 11 astronauts Neil Armstrong and Edwin "Buzz" Aldrin became the first men to set foot on the Moon. This unlikely-looking Lunar Landing Module accomplished its job admirably—taking them to the surface and bringing them back to the orbiting Apollo spacecraft. Its two main parts are made of aluminum with titanium fittings to save weight. The lower or descent stage has one rocket engine (1), which can be throttled from about 1000 to 10,000 pounds thrust. It uses Aerozene 50 fuel with nitrogen tetroxide oxidizer. Around the engine are the four main propellant tanks, scientific equipment, life support, electrical system batteries, helium, oxygen, and water tanks.

Atop the descent stage is the ascent stage, also with one main engine. It also has four sets of reaction control system thrusters (2) which can operate in redundant independent pairs. On top is the docking adapter (3), linking the Lunar Landing Module to the parent ship which takes the astronauts home. It is surrounded by an array of antennas for rendezvous radar, S-band, VHF, and lunar surface communications. During their one to three days on the Moon, crews existed in a scant 235 cubic feet of pressurized volume. The Module was so well designed it was able to provide life support and save the astronauts of the crippled Apollo 13.

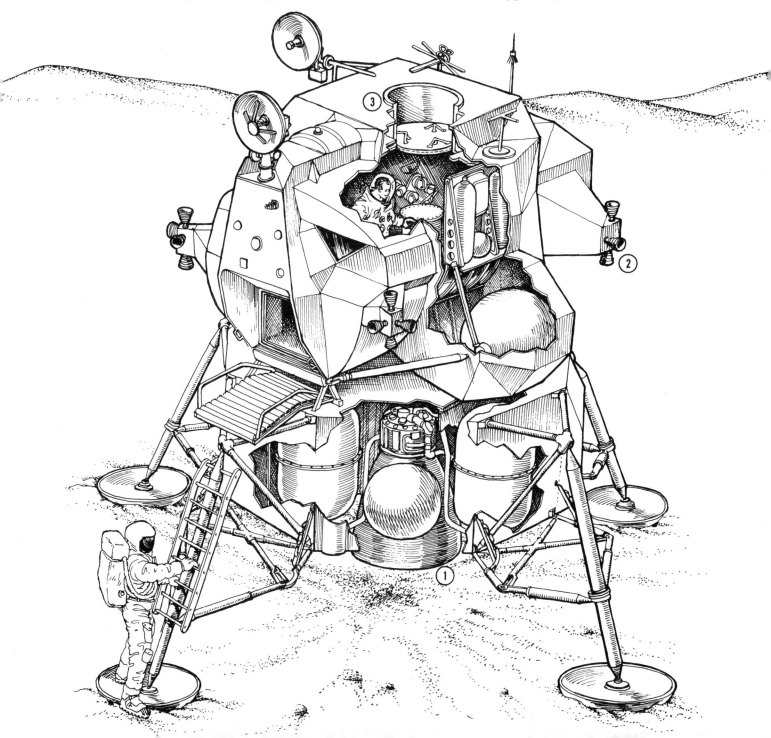

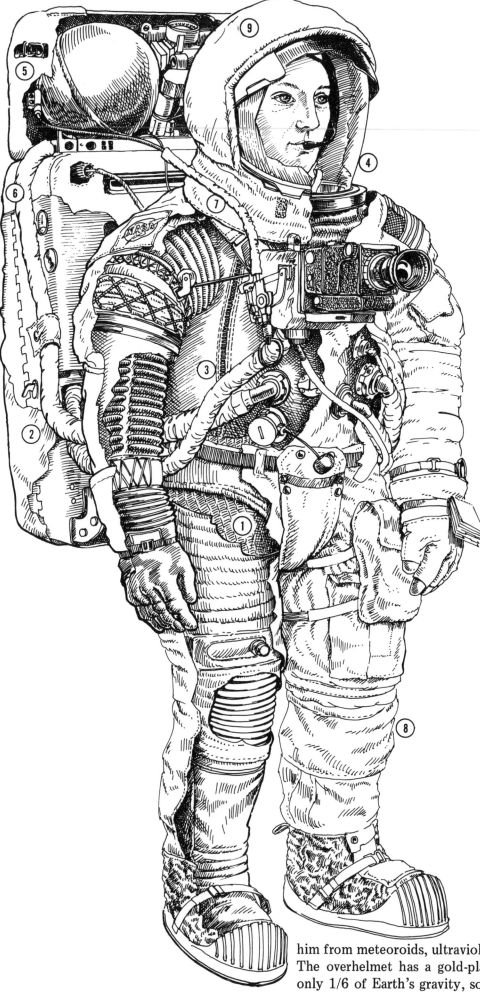

This space suit is actually three suits in one, each custom tailored to fit the astronaut, and all necessary to keep him alive in the hostile lunar environment. The Moon has no water or oxygen. With no atmospheric pressure, exposed body fluids would boil. Temperatures range from 250° F during the 340 hour lunar day to 250° below zero in the equally long night. Radiation and micrometeoroids are additional hazards.

The innermost suit (1) is a mesh of fabric and water-cooled tubes, connected to the portable life-support system (PLSS) backpack (2), from which water and oxygen are precisely metered. Next comes the pressure suit (3) constructed of fabric and rubber, and the pressure helmet (4). These too are linked to the PLSS, which removes carbon dioxide and other contaminants from the oxygen stream. A chest-mounted remote control unit permits the astronaut to adjust oxygen flow and cooling temperature to his liking. The PLSS will sustain activity for up to eight hours. A separate oxygen system (5) is available for an emergency, connected through the emergency oxygen umbilical (6) and operated with the actuator (7).

The astronaut is equipped with a sheath urinal and collection bag; no provision can be made for bowel movements other than absorbent underwear. (Sealable disposable bags are used in the spacecraft.) Within his helmet he has a compressed food bar to nibble on, a tube for sipping a beverage from a suspended bag, and a microphone to communicate with his fellow astronaut and Mission Control. The outer suit protects him from meteoroids, ultraviolet rays, dirt, and other radiations. The overhelmet has a gold-plated sunvisor (9). The Moon has only 1/6 of Earth's gravity, so all this equipment is light there.

Thanks to a small electric cart called the Lunar Rover, the astronauts of the last three Apollo missions saw much more of the Moon than just the area around their landing module. For safety reasons they drove no further than the six miles they could have walked back if the cart failed: even so, they covered ten times the territory they would have seen on foot.

The two-seated vehicle weighed 462 pounds—only 77 pounds in lunar gravity. Each wheel was powered by two silver-zinc batteries driving a one-quarter horsepower motor: top speed was about seven miles an hour, but the Rover could climb and descend slopes of 25°.

The Lunar Rover arrived folded up on the side of the Lunar Landing Module descent stage. Its clever hinges, springs, and locks let it practically put itself together as it was unpacked. It is equipped with a high-gain antenna (1) for communicating with Mission Control on Earth; an omnidirectional low gain antenna (2); a television camera (3); a 16 millimeter movie camera (4); a display console and hand control (5); stowage for tools, scientific equipment, and sample collection bags (6); and wire mesh tires (7).

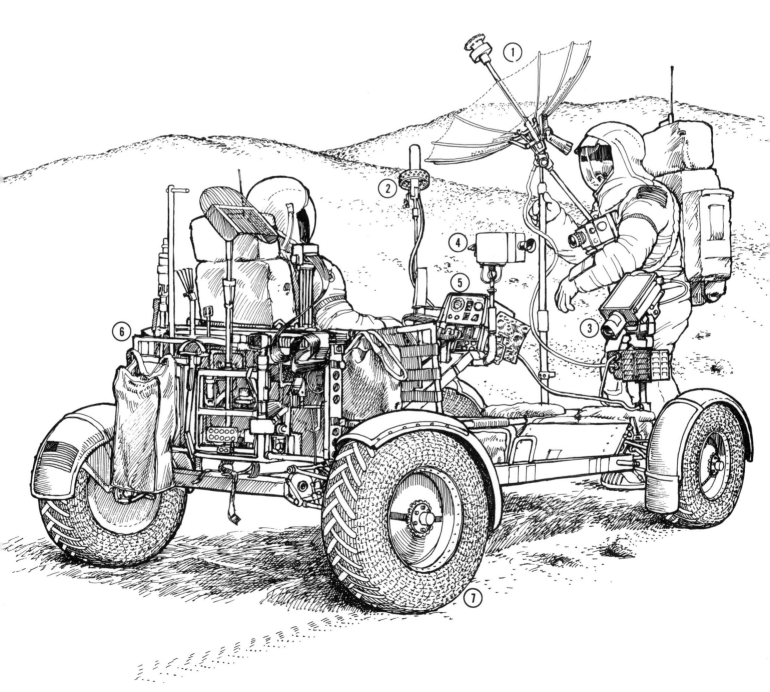

All U.S. manned flights except for the Space Shuttle have ended in the sea, allowing a wide choice of landing spots without danger to inhabited areas. An Apollo spacecraft approaches the Earth at nearly 25,000 miles an hour, 60 hours after leaving a lunar orbit at 5600 miles per hour. Mid-course corrections using data from ground stations prepare for reentry. Accuracy is vital, since if the craft enters the atmosphere at too steep an angle, it would burn from atmospheric friction like a meteor; too shallow an angle could let the craft skip off the atmosphere like a stone on a pond, back into space. The safe path lies in a corridor about 25 miles thick.

Fifteen minutes before entering the atmosphere, the Apollo Command Module separates from its Service Module, and turns its blunt bottom forward: its heat shield must protect the craft from frictional heating temperatures as high as 5000° F. Once the entry into the atmosphere begins (1), the commander can alter its course somewhat over the 5000 miles of its entry path. At 15,000 feet three ringsail landing parachutes open (2), dropping off when the craft hits the water.

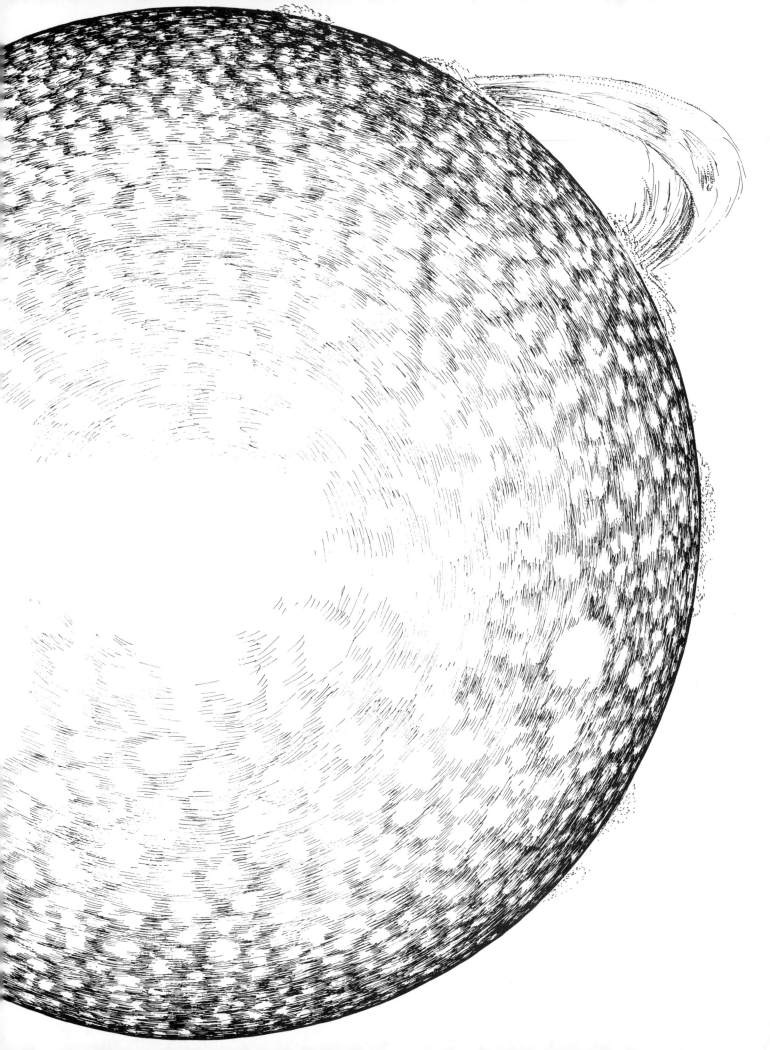

The awesome scale of the solar system makes exploration beyond the Moon very difficult. Here we show the Sun (on the left) and the planets with their relative sizes correct. But if the Sun and planets were reduced to this size, the nearest planet to the Sun, Mercury, would still be 35 feet from it; Venus would be 30 feet further, the Earth and the Moon 25 feet still further, and Mars another 50 feet. Jupiter, 475 feet from the Sun, would be 335 feet beyond Mars; Saturn would be 875 feet from the Sun, Uranus 1750, Neptune 2750, and Pluto 3600 feet. Representing planetary distances in this scale would be like using a basketball for the Sun and a BB for Pluto over half a mile away.

The inner planets—Mercury through Mars—are much denser, made up of heavier atomic elements. The outer planets are formed of lighter elements, such as hydrogen and helium. As a result, Saturn, the second-largest planet, has a surface gravity barely greater than that of the Earth. Refer to the table below for other comparisons.

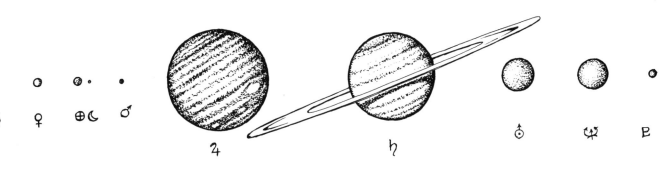

SOLAR SYSTEM

Planet	Symbol	Distance from the Sun		Diameter		Number Satellites	Surface Gravity (g)	Period in Years
		AU*	Kilometers	Relative to Earth	Kilometers			
(Sun)	☉	0	0	109	1.396×10^6	(9)	28	—
Mercury	☿	0.387	5.79×10^7	0.38	4.84×10^3	0	0.380	0.241
Venus	♀	0.723	1.08×10^8	0.97	12.1×10^3	0	0.893	0.616
Earth	⊕	1.00	1.496×10^8	1.00	12.76×10^3	1	1.00	1.00
Moon	☽	—	—	0.27	3.476×10^3	0	0.165	0.075
Mars	♂	1.52	2.27×10^8	0.52	6.82×10^3	2	0.377	1.88
Jupiter	♃	5.20	7.78×10^8	11.0	14.28×10^4	16	2.54	11.9
Saturn	♄	9.54	1.43×10^9	9.03	12.08×10^4	17	1.06	29.5
Uranus	♅	19.2	2.87×10^9	3.72	4.70×10^4	15	1.07	84
Neptune	♆	30.1	4.50×10^9	3.38	4.46×10^4	3	1.4	165
Pluto	♇	39.5	5.91×10^9	1.02	1.4×10^3	0	0.7	248

* 1 AU = 1.496×10^8 km = 92,959,670 miles = distance from the Earth to the Sun.

With the Mariner missions the U.S. began looking at other planets. Mariner 1 failed, but Mariner 2 made a successful passage of Venus December 14, 1962, discovering an unexpected surface temperature of 800° F, which seemed to eliminate the possibility of life there. Mariner 3, the first craft aimed at Mars, also failed, but on November 28, 1964, an Atlas-Agena D launched Mariner 4. The 575-pound spacecraft arrived at Mars seven and a half months later; during its fly-by it took 21 pictures which showed Mars to be a dry, crater-covered desert. Mariners 6 and 7, identical 910-pound spacecraft, arrived at Mars July 30 and August 4, 1969. During their fly-by they took 200 pictures, with much greater detail than those of Mariner 4—3.9 million bits of data per picture, as opposed to Mariner 4's 240,000 bits. Mariner 9, sent off towards a Mars orbit May 30, 1971, arrived November 13; much more of the surface could be photographed from orbit than a fly-by permitted. At first dust storms hid the surface but after two months the dust cleared, revealing a system of canyons many times greater than the Grand Canyon.

Mariner 9 weighed 2272 pounds, with 4 rectangular solar panels (1) spanning 22½ feet. In the central section were two propellant tanks (2) and the thruster (3). Television cameras were located below (4), with high (5), medium (6), and low (7) gain antennas above.

The Soviet Union has launched probes at Mars or Venus nearly every opportunity since 1960 that planetary positions made such flights possible. Their first Venus probe, Venera 1, reached Venus in May 1961, but failed to send information back. Venera 2's communications also failed in February 1966, and a capsule ejected from Venera 3 was calculated to have hit Venus, but it sent no data.

Venera 4 penetrated the atmosphere of Venus October 18, 1967, and reported high temperatures and pressures; 5 and 6 reached Venus May 16 and 17, 1969. They reported surface temperature around 750° F and a pressure of 60 Earth atmospheres. Venera 8, arriving July 22, 1972, had special cooling equipment which enabled it to become the first capsule to transmit usable data from Venus's surface.

Venera 9, launched June 8, 1975, took the first pictures of the surface-a rocky landscape rather like Mars and the Moon. Venera 10, launched 6 days later, repeated this success. Each had a propulsion unit (1) attached to one end, the landing capsule was at the other (2). The landing capsule (3) has deployed, with its cover (4) separated by small rockets. The lander is about 10½ feet long, 3 feet in diameter. A high gain antenna (5) remains oriented towards Earth while the solar panels (6) face the Sun. Two low gain antennas (7) keep contact with the landing capsule.

Pioneer 10, the first man-made object to travel near Jupiter, is also the first object to have been sent out of the solar system by man. Pioneer 11 was the first man-made object to approach Saturn. Launched in 1972 and 1973 with Atlas-Centaur boosters and a third upper stage, these 550-pound craft used a direct ascent trajectory with no parking orbit to achieve the highest velocity of any man-made object—about 32,000 miles per hour. They took 21 months to reach Jupiter.

Each craft has a large communications antenna (1), two distended radioisotope thermo-electric generators (2), and a magnetometer isolated 17 feet away on a boom (3). Behind the

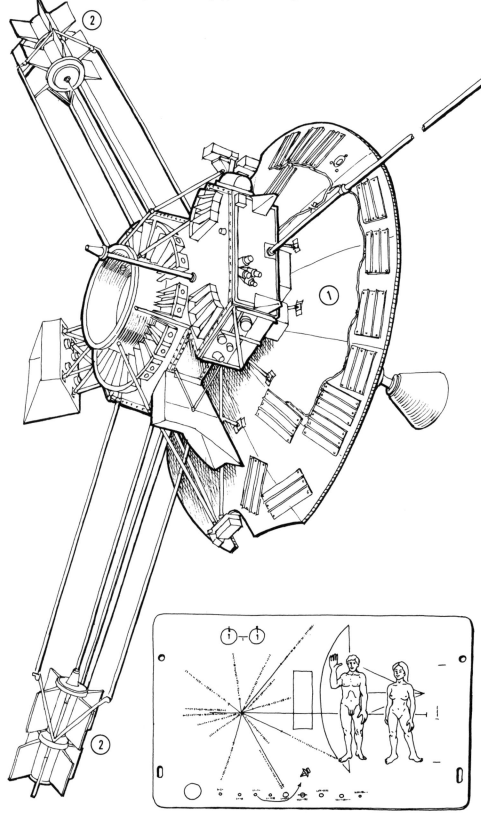

antenna are the main equipment compartment and the booster attachment ring. The craft spins around the centerline of the antenna to maintain pointing stability. Pioneer 10 measured Jupiter's magnetic field and the charged particles trapped in that field. Thermal and visible images of the planet were obtained, and coded signals of each image sent back to Earth with 8 watts of power. The signal travels the 500 million miles at the speed of light, taking 45 minutes.

A 6x9-inch gold anodized aluminum plate attached to the spacecraft will tell its origin to any finder beyond the solar system. It shows a man and woman in front of a silhouette of the craft, to show their size, and shows the woman's height as a multiple of the hydrogen wavelength. A radial pattern with binary number codes indicates the position of the sun relative to 14 pulsars and the center of our galaxy.

July 20, 1976—7 years after the Apollo astronauts set foot on the Moon—the Viking 1 lander settled on the Martian surface. A month later Viking 2 landed 4600 miles away. The Viking spacecraft is a mobile laboratory, conducting experiments in geology, microbiology, and meteorology. In Mars orbit the lander was released from the orbiter (1) by an automatic sequence; then the heat shield was jettisoned, the parachute opened, retro-rockets (2) fired, and the craft landed. Once down, the craft deploys its S-band high gain antenna (3) to communicate with Earth. An extendable boom (4) gathers specimens for analysis in the test chambers (5); twin cameras take pictures of the landscape (6). Also visible are the VHF antenna (7), the meteorology sensors (8), and the descent propellant tanks (9).

Viking found the Martian atmosphere to be 96% carbon dioxide, and so tenuous (less than 1% of Earth's) that liquid water would vaporize instantly on Mars. Although many elements necessary for life are present, no evidence of life was found.

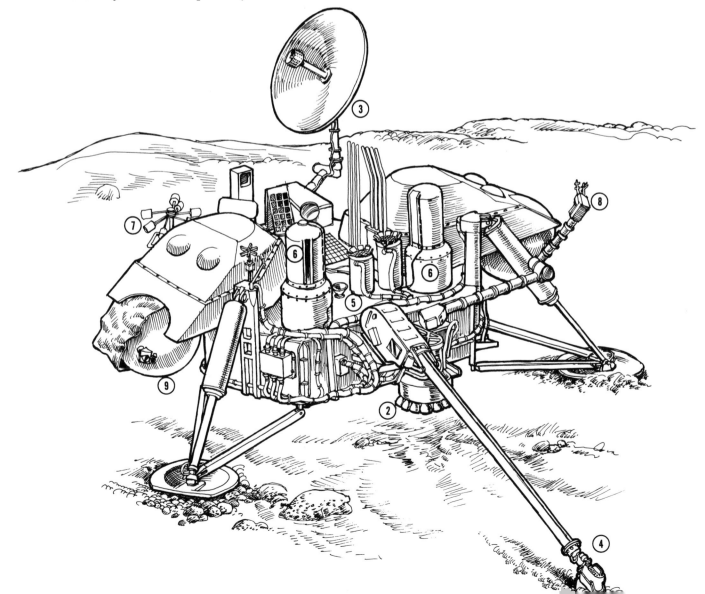

Jupiter, the Sun's largest planet, is eleven times the diameter of the Earth and five times the Earth's distance from the Sun. Four of Jupiter's moons are about the size of the Earth's moon. Ganymede, the largest, is slightly bigger than Mercury. Its ice crust is marked with craters and grooves. Callisto is completely covered with craters. Europa, on the other hand, has the smoothest surface yet found in the solar system, but its ice crust is laced with cracks many miles wide. Io (shown in the foreground) is the only known volcanically active body in the solar system. It is composed of sulfur and silicate.

Jupiter is a dynamic planet. Its turbulent surface of swirling hydrogen and helium gas rotates at slightly different speeds as the planet turns once every 9 hours and 55 minutes. The upper layers of the atmosphere are relatively cold (estimates vary from 10° F to 55,000° F below zero), but planetary models indicate a very hot interior (perhaps 25,000° F to 55,000° F).

The two Voyager spacecraft which passed Jupiter in 1979 relayed information on the newly-discovered thin ring of micron-sized particles; Jupiter's strong magnetic field; the auroras in the polar regions; and the donut-shaped plasma of ionized sulphur and oxygen in Io's orbit path.

The Voyager 1 spacecraft, launched on a Titan III Centaur rocket booster, carried two T.V. cameras and nine other science packages past Jupiter and to within 77,000 miles of Saturn's cloud tops on November 12, 1980. Using 380 watts of power from three radioisotope thermoelectric generators, the twelve-foot dish antenna radioed pictures and data nearly one billion miles back to Earth. Scientists found Saturn to be like Jupiter, with turbulent bands composed of nine-tenths hydrogen and one-tenth helium gas. However, the bands are partly obscured by a high-altitude layer of ammonia haze.

It was understood before Pioneer and Voyager arrived that the rings of Saturn must be composed of multitudes of particles. Each particle, from dust size to boulder size, has established its own individual orbit after eons of collision and adjustment. Voyager showed this equilibrium to be in the form of hundreds, if not thousands, of small rings, rather than the smooth discs which appear through Earth telescopes. Also, within the rings were discovered several small satellites which seem to play a part in shaping the rings.

Saturn's largest moon, Titan, rivals Mercury and Ganymede in size. Its surface is obscured by a nitrogen atmosphere with many times the thickness and twice the surface pressure of the Earth's atmosphere. The surface is suspected to be about 300° F below zero.

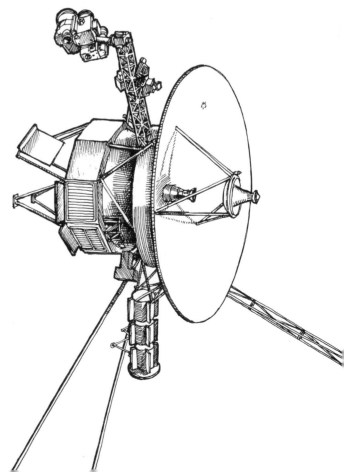

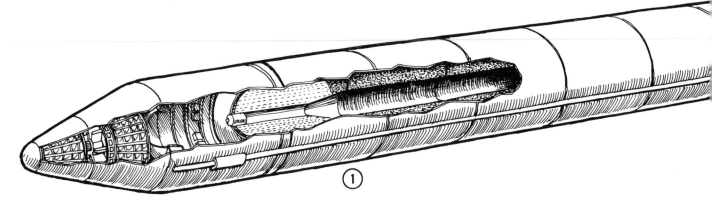

The Space Shuttle, flown since 1981, is the first launch vehicle designed to be reusable, thereby reducing the cost of putting payloads into orbit. As many as 10 people can be carried, though the Shuttle is designed for a crew of 4. An ordinary mission would last 7 days in orbit, but with proper provisioning could be extended to a month.

Two slender solid propellant boosters (1) each carry a million pounds of fuel and develop two and a half million pounds of thrust at launch. The large central tank carries liquid oxygen (2) and liquid hydrogen (3) fed through pipes to the main engines (4) on the orbiter (5). Twenty-seven miles above the Earth the solid propellants finish burning, and the rocket shells are parachuted back to the sea 150 miles from the launch point; they will be collected and reused. The liquid propellant tank, empty by the time the Shuttle goes into orbit, falls into the sea and is lost.

When the Shuttle has completed its mission it slows down with retro-rockets to leave orbit and reenter the atmosphere. The nose, leading wing edges, and belly are protected from atmospheric friction with heat-resistant ceramic tiles. The Shuttle can land on a conventional type jet runway.

The shuttle orbiter is 122.3 feet long, with a 78-foot wing span. Its cargo bay (6) is 15 by 60 feet. The entire assemblage is 184.2 feet long, and weighs 2200 tons at launch with full fuel load.

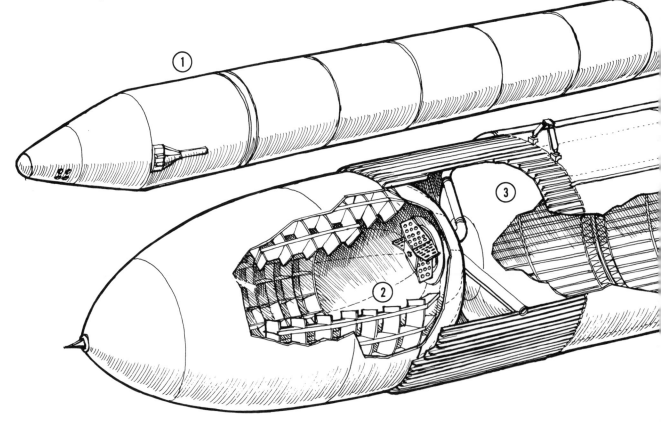

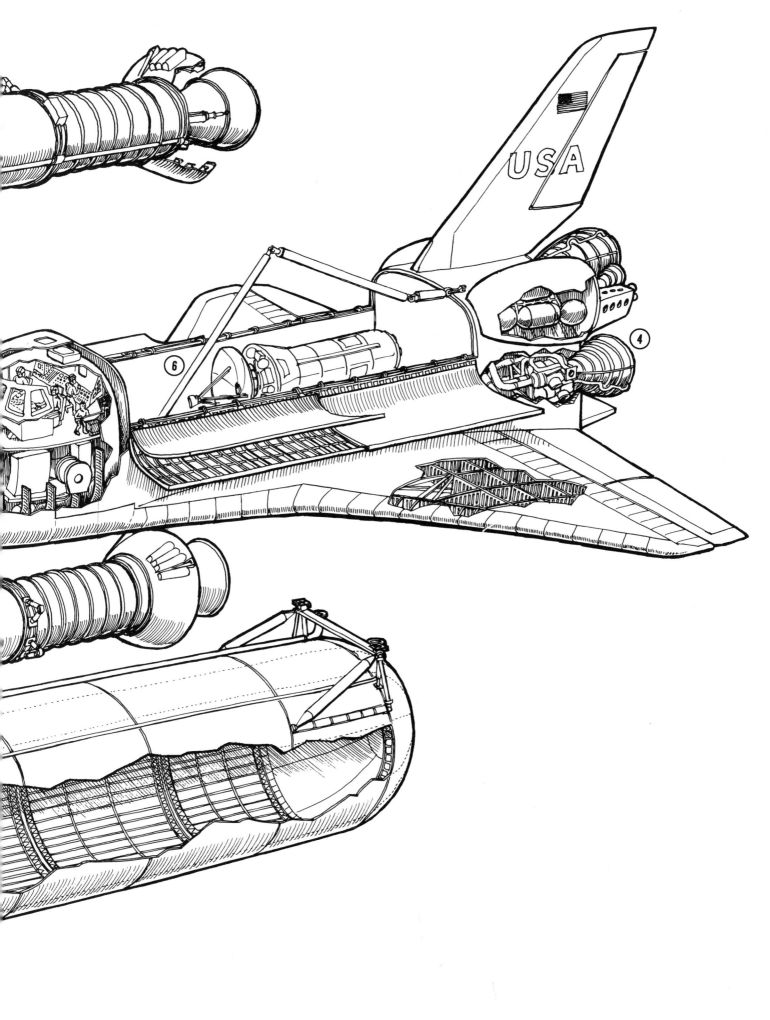

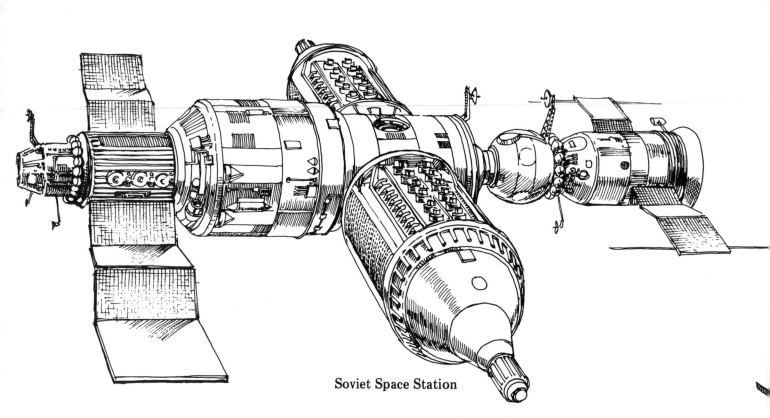

Soviet Space Station

The new Soviet space station became a reality on February 20, 1986 with the launch of the core module, called Mir for "peace," from the Baikonur Cosmodrome. The Mir module is a physical outgrowth of the earlier Salyut vehicle family. It is about 40 feet long, 14 feet in diameter, and weighs about 20 tons. It was launched with the standard Proton booster. One end of the Mir module sprouts solar cells for electrical power generation; attached to the other end is a docking module with four side ports and one end port. To the end port is docked the Soyuz-T crew transport and supply vehicle. The side ports can house a variety of laboratory facilities, such as the Kosmos vehicles shown here with their conical payload return modules. The central Mir core is thus reserved for crew support and living quarters.

The laboratory modules will be devoted to such things as astrophysics, biology, materials processing research, astronomy, high-energy X-ray experiments, and Earth surveys. The modules, each of comparable size to Mir, can remain linked to the core for months, or fly in parallel orbits until they are ready for refurbishment and resupply.

On March 13, Cosmonauts Kizim and Solovyov were sent aloft in their Soyuz T-15 to activate the new space platform. The event marked the beginning of the world's first continuously staffed space station. The new system has all new life support systems, interior, and living quarters. There is a control console and a dining area, as well as a small repair shop with a steel table, vises, soldering equipment, and tools. Crew members have separate cabins or cubicals, each equipped with a folding chair, a desk, a mirror, and a sleeping bag. The common area features a dining table, a buffet built into a storage locker, and exercise equipment.

The Soviets clearly intend to continue to push space endurance records beyond their current 237-day record, perhaps in preparation for the first manned expedition to Mars. Past experience indicates that mission durations greater than three or four months produce tremendous physical and psychological pressures, after which fatigue and stress mount dangerously. Crews will undoubtedly be rotated extensively, while experimental animals are left on board for observation over longer durations.

Space Telescope

Named for the famous astronomer, the Edwin P. Hubble Space Telescope was dreamed of for decades before it was finally placed in orbit on April 25, 1990. It operates much the same way as a ground based telescope. Its central cylindrical body houses a system of mirrors, like a standard reflector telescope. But, flying high above the diffusion and distortion caused by the Earth's atmosphere, it will produce a brighter and sharper image. Its promise, however, is yet to be realized; a spherical aberration in the 94.5-inch mirror made it impossible to focus the telescope clearly after it was launched. Some of the experiments the telescope was designed to perform, such as analyzing visible and ultraviolet light from celestial bodies, can still be made. Others, in particular long looks far into the reaches of space, must await "surgery" to be performed from the space shuttle.

The Space Station

The United States Space Station, orbiting the Earth at an altitude of 220 to 250 miles, will be a microgravity research facility, an earth and space observation post, a satellite service and repair center, an assembly point for automated inter-planetary vehicles, a staging base for human expeditions to the Moon and Mars, and a proof of concept facility for future space habitation and colonization. As currently envisioned, it will become operational in the mid 1990s, beginning with a crew of about eight astronauts and scientists. The inhabited portion of the Space Station will be made up of a cluster of cylindrical modules joined together with a system of docking spheres and tunnels. Each module will be about 14 feet in diameter and 45 feet long, consistent with Shuttle launch capabilities. This cluster of modules will hang in the middle of a lightweight framework of beams and girders which also support several hundred square feet of solar panels, satellite and rocket servicing garages, space-pointed telescopes, and Earth pointed sensors and antennas. The total structure will stretch about 500 feet. It will require about fifteen Shuttle launches to build, and a number of other launches to supply equipment. Additional launches, at least every ninety days, will be required to rotate the crew, bring food, water, and other supplies, and return scientific specimens and waste materials to the ground.

The first U.S. Space Station will not spin or rotate in order to provide artificial gravity for the crew. There are two reasons: first, many scientists want to investigate the effects of removing gravity, and second, a spinning station would complicate docking maneuvers and make antenna and telescope pointing more difficult. Future stations may rotate or have spinning sections for the comfort of the crew and to help prevent some of the bone and muscle losses caused by low gravity levels.

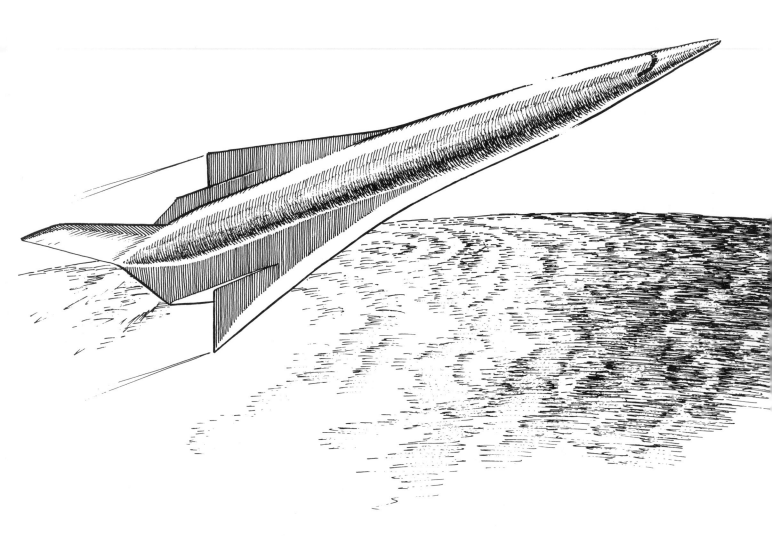

Aerospace Plane

The aerospace plane is a superspeed (hypersonic) global transport, a long-range air defense interceptor, and a launch vehicle. It will someday carry payloads to orbit, leaving from and returning to conventional airport runways. The success of this concept depends on the advancement of several sophisticated technologies, including propulsion systems, structures and materials, heat shielding, and control systems. Once developed, however, it will be more economical to use than the Shuttle or other launch vehicles, because it will not require extensive launch facilities and ground crews. Furthermore, it will be entirely reuseable.

The aerospace plane will reach speeds of 4000-20,000 miles per hour (Mach 6 to 25) and altitudes of 100,000 to 350,000 feet. It will be fueled with liquid hydrogen, which will occupy much of its internal volume. Unlike other launch vehicles that carry liquid oxygen or other oxidizers, the aerospace plane will scoop oxygen from the atmosphere to burn the hydrogen. As an Earth transport, the aerospace plane could carry passengers or cargo half way around the world in an hour. It may be developed before the end of the century.

ROCKET MILESTONES

Date	Name	Country	Weight	Description
c. 1000 AD		China		Gunpowder developed.
1200s		China		Fire arrows in widespread use
Mar 16, 1926		U.S.		First liquid-fuel rocket launch
Oct 3, 1942	V-2	Germany		First successful V-2 rocket launch.
Oct 4, 1957	Sputnik 1	U.S.S.R.	184 lb	First man-made satellite.
Nov 3, 1957	Sputnik 2	U.S.S.R.	1,121 lb	First orbiting animal (dog Laika).
Jan 31, 1958	Explorer 1	U.S.	31 lb	First U.S. satellite, discovered Van Allen belt.
Jan 7, 1959	Luna 1	U.S.S.R.	797 lb	First vehicle to achieve solar orbit. Passed within 3728 miles of Moon.
Aug 7, 1959	Explorer 6	U.S.		First photo of Earth from space.
Sep 12, 1959	Luna 2	U.S.S.R.	860 lb	First probe to hit Moon.
Oct 4, 1959	Luna 3	U.S.S.R.	614 lb	First photos of Moon's backside.
Aug 12, 1960	Echo 1	U.S.	156 lb	First passive (reflector) communications satellite.
Aug 19, 1960	Sputnik 5	U.S.S.R.	10,141 lb	First live orbital recovery (two dogs).
Oct 4, 1960	Courier 1B	U.S.	500 lb	First active repeater communications satellite.
Apr 12, 1961	Vostok 1	U.S.S.R.	10,417 lb	First manned spaceflight; Gagarin recovered after one orbit.
May 5, 1961	Mercury Freedom 7	U.S.	2,845 lb	First American in space, Shepard, sub-orbital flight.
Nov 29, 1961	Mercury 5	U.S.	2,900 lb	First U.S. live orbital flight. Chimpanzee recovered after two orbits.
Feb 20, 1962	Mercury Friendship 7	U.S.	2,987 lb	First U. S. manned orbital flight. Glenn, three orbits.
Apr 23, 1962	Ranger 4	U.S.	730 lb	First U.S. Moon impact.
Aug 25, 1962	Mariner 2	U.S.	447 lb	First successful Venus fly-by.
Jun 16, 1963	Vostok 6	U.S.S.R.	10,390 lb	First woman in space: Tereshkova. Passed within three miles of Vostok 5. Landed by parachute after 48 orbits.
Jul 30, 1964	Ranger 7	U.S.	806 lb	Impacted Moon; returned 4308 pictures.
Oct 12, 1964	Voskhod 1	U.S.S.R.	11,728 lb	First three-man crew: Komarov, Feokistov, Yegorov.
Mar 18, 1965	Voskhod 2	U.S.S.R.	12,527 lb	Leonov performs first space walk, 20 minutes, 17 orbits.
Mar 23, 1965	Gemini 3	U.S.	7,111 lb	First of Gemini manned orbital maneuvers; Grissom, Young; three orbits.
Jul 16, 1965	Proton I	U.S.S.R.	26,896 lb	U. S. S. R. physics "lab"

ROCKET MILESTONES (Continued)

Date	Name	Country	Weight	Description
Nov 16, 1965	Venera 3	U.S.S.R.	2,116 lb	Impacted Venus March 1, 1966; failed to return data.
Dec 4, 1965	Gemini 7	U.S.	8,076 lb	Record 220 orbits, 330.6 hours; Borman, Lovell.
Dec 15, 1965	Gemini 6	U.S.	7,817 lb	Rendezvous to within one foot of Gemini 7; Schirra, Stafford; 17 orbits.
Jan 31, 1966	Luna 9	U.S.S.R.	3,490 lb	First lunar soft landing. Returned photos of surface.
Mar 16, 1966	Gemini 8	U.S.	8,351 lb	First in orbit docking test (with Gemini 8 target); Armstrong, Scott; 6.5 orbits.
Mar 31, 1966	Luna 10	U.S.S.R.	3,527 lb	First lunar orbit.
Aug 10, 1966	Lunar Orbiter I	U.S.	853 lb	Photographed Moon until August 29, 1966.
Sep 12, 1966	Gemini 11	U.S.	8,374 lb	First docking in first orbit. Conrad, Gordon; 47 orbits.
Apr 17, 1967	Surveyor 3	U.S.	625 lb	Landed on Moon. Took photos, made soil analysis.
Nov 7, 1967	Surveyor 6	U.S.	617 lb	Performed first rocket lift-off from Moon.
Nov 9, 1967	Apollo 4	U.S.		First successful Apollo flight —unmanned.
Jan 22, 1968	Apollo 5	U.S.	31,700 lb	First flight of Lunar Module —unmanned.
Sep 15, 1968	Zond 5	U.S.S.R.		First lunar fly-around—recovered from Indian Ocean.
Oct 11, 1968	Apollo 7	U.S.	45,089 lb	First manned Apollo flight. Schirra, Cunningham, Eisele; 163 orbits.
Nov 10, 1968	Zond 6	U.S.S.R.		Circumlunar flight landed in U.S.S.R. after aerodynamic glide reentry.
Dec 21, 1968	Apollo 8	U.S.	63,650 lb	First manned circumlunar flight. Borman, Lovell, and Anders; 10 lunar orbits, 147 hours.
Jan 14, 1969	Soyuz 4	U.S.S.R.	14,000 lb	First link-up of two manned vehicles. First manned return in other than launched vehicle.
Jan 15, 1969	Soyuz 5	U.S.S.R.	14,000 lb	Khrunov, Yeliseyev, and Volynov.
Feb 24, 1969	Mariner 6	U.S.	910 lb	Flew by Mars at 2120 miles on July 31, 1969, sending 75 television pictures.
Mar 3, 1969	Apollo 9	U.S.	80,585 lb	First successful manned Apollo flight with lunar module; 151 orbits, 241.9 hours, 40 minutes EVA.